T0366044

Centered

Inspiration from the hands of the potter

Print information available on the last page

Rev. date: 08/31/2018

To order additional copies of this book, contact:
Xlibris
1-888-795-4274
www.Xlibris.com
Orders@Xlibris.com

Centered

Inspiration from the hands of the potter

by

Terance and Anita Painter

Trudging down a dusty path, his way made weary by a heavy heart, went a man looking for answers. So it was that out of the bustle of everyday life Jeremiah was led by God to seek the quiet realm of the artist at work.

"Go down to the potter's house,
and there I will give you my message."

Jeremiah 18:2

3

Outside the potter's house are great mounds of clay, dug by hand, breaking down for use by natural processes, and allowed to weather and age. It is without form, organization, and in a state of chaos. These small particles are lacking in purpose; still, clay contains the same elements that are found in the earth and man, only it can achieve nothing by itself.

The Lord God formed the man from the dust of the ground and breathed into his nostrils the breath of life, and man became a living being.

Genesis 2:7

5

Overwhelmed and desperately needing a direction, Jeremiah entered the potter's house to gain a better opportunity to focus and hear God's word. How many times have we, even as Christians, been overwhelmed, concerned over loved ones, or lost ourselves? If we listened closely, where would God send us?...To the potter's house?...Into the quiet to find him?...And, if He spoke, would we be able to hear what He had to say?

"Be still, and know that I am God…"

Psalm 46:10

As Jeremiah contemplated the condition of his people, he was possibly greeted as a friend by a family of workers all doing their part toward a purpose, striving in unison toward a shared goal, not their own.

A reminder to us – we are a family of Christians, working toward God's purpose, not our own.

"Every kingdom divided against itself will be ruined, and every city or household divided against itself will not stand."

Matthew 12:25

Left alone clay would dry out and crack, never fulfilling its potential. This is not the potter's intent. Organization is no accident. Even before the forming, there is a plan.

"For I know the plans I have for you," declares the Lord, "plans to prosper you and not to harm you, plans to give you hope and a future."

Jeremiah 29:11

The potter begins his craft by removing gravel, sticks, and impurities that would get in the way of the clay being formed for something useful. Hard and inflexible parts must be cast aside or reworked.

8

Evil tries to limit us by making us feel unworthy. But God knew of our sin even before we were born and still found us worth the price. So why do we question our purpose or value?

The potter organizes the clay by wedging (pulling, stretching, and kneading), requiring force and pressure. Wedging homogenizes the clay and removes air pockets that would deform the vessel. As clay is worked, it spirals inward like a conch shell.

Preparing clay was a job handed down from father to son.

"For God sent not his Son into the world to condemn the world, but that the world through him might be saved."

John 3:17

There are so many ways that we feel pulled and stretched by this world – its only intent to pull us apart. When God stretches us, He's organizing and preparing us for a purpose, though the avenues it takes for Him to get us where we need to be aren't always easy to accept.

"No eye has seen,

no ear has heard,

no mind has conceived

what God has prepared for those who love him."

1 Corinthians 2:9

11

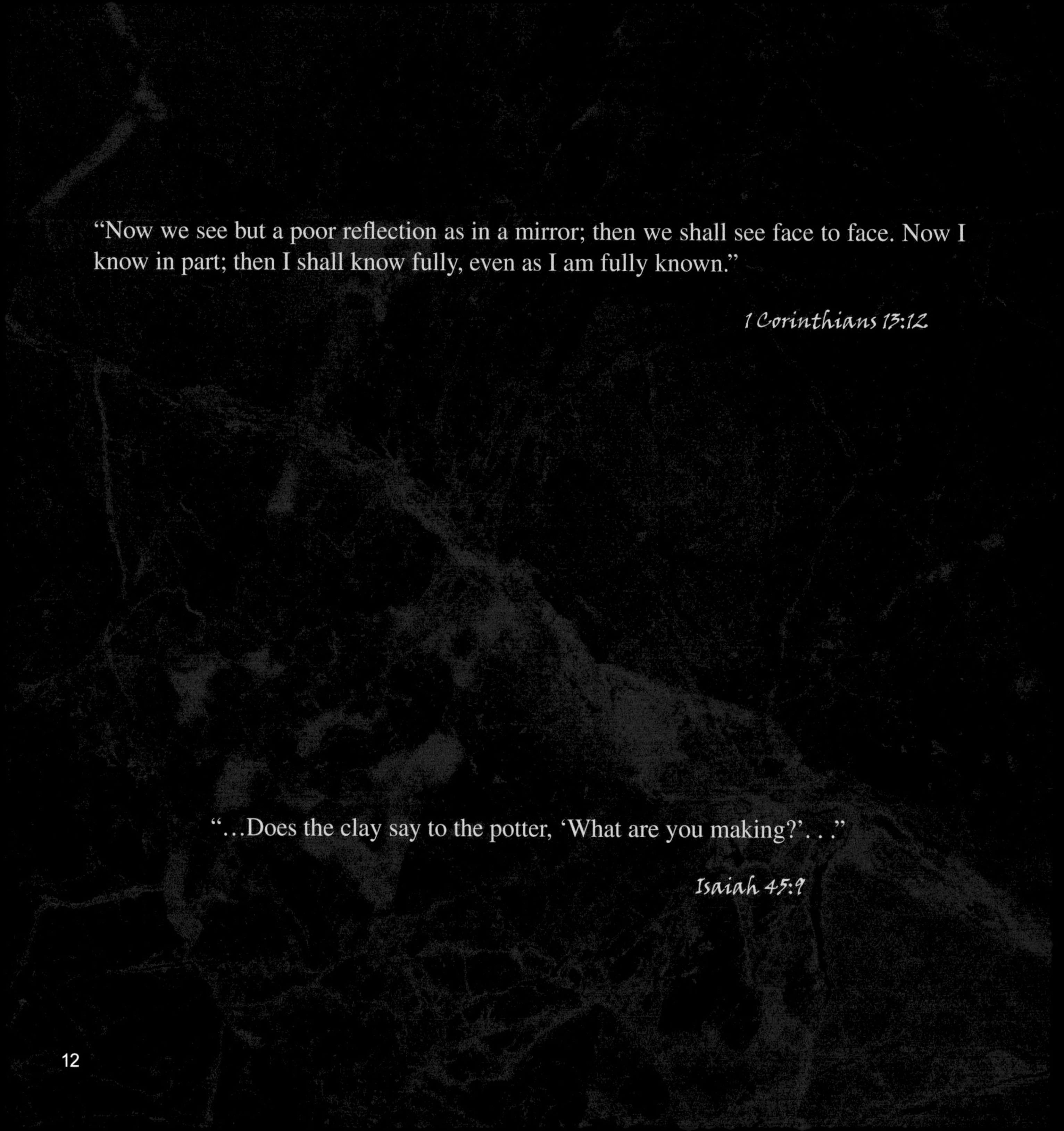

"Now we see but a poor reflection as in a mirror; then we shall see face to face. Now I know in part; then I shall know fully, even as I am fully known."

1 Corinthians 13:12

"...Does the clay say to the potter, 'What are you making?'..."

Isaiah 45:9

"For my thoughts are not your thoughts, neither are your ways my ways," declares the Lord.

Isaiah 55:8

*T*he potter goes to the wheel and begins centering. This process requires water and pressure to shape the clay, as it spins, into a uniform, symmetrical dome at the exact center of the wheel. Without this step the form would be misshapen and lopsided, never becoming what it should be. Centering is crucial.

"…for it is God who works in you to will and to act according to his good purpose."

Philippians 2:13

Centering is equally important for us – finding our way from daily distractions so we can center our lives on God and become all He wants us to be.

The process of making a vessel on the potter's wheel is called "throwing". Throwing would not be possible without water. It eases the friction between the clay and the potter's hands. Water is essential.

"Sir," the woman said, "you have nothing to draw with and the well is deep. Where can you get this living water?" …Jesus answered, "Everyone who drinks this water will be thirsty again, but whoever drinks the water I give him will never thirst…"

The potter penetrates to the heart of the clay and opens it up, establishing a firm foundation to support what is to come.

Fear not, I am with thee; O be not dismayed,
For I am thy God, and will still give thee aid;
I'll strengthen thee, help thee, and cause thee to stand,
Upheld by my righteous, omnipotent hand.

"How Firm a Foundation"   George Keith

Clay possesses the unique ability to capture and hold form. When it is touched by the potter, it is forever changed.

Our lives should show evidence of God at work in us. Though not perfected, we continue to strive and to hope.

Have Thine own way, Lord.
Have Thine own way.
Thou art the potter. I am the clay.
Mould me and make me
after Thy will,…
while I am waiting, yielded and still.

"Have Thine Own Way, Lord"

Adelaide A. Pollard

Now faith is the substance of things hoped for,
the evidence of things not seen.

Hebrews 11:1

There is a soothing fascination in watching an artist at work, a clearing of the mind. We are comforted by the ritual of the movement and yet aware of something greater about to take place.

Brothers, I do not consider myself
yet to have taken hold of it. But one
thing I do: Forgetting what is behind
and straining toward what is ahead, I
press on toward the goal to win the
prize for which God has called me
heavenward in Christ Jesus.

Philippians 3:13-14

Now it is time for growth- all the way to the bottom and pulling upward.

The potter can't form the vessel with one hand on the outside only. Outside pressure would cause it to collapse. One hand must go into the heart of the vessel while the other, on the outside, holds the shape.

I can do all things through Christ, who strengtheneth me.

Philippians 4:13

Reaching deep within, the potter makes pass after pass. Nothing happens in one easy movement yet he returns again and again. Each succeeding path of his fingers begins to bring the vessel into shape, a continual effort to strive and perfect.

The pressures of the outside world can often become too much to bear. We cannot be Christians on the outside only, or we, too, will collapse. We must return again and again in prayer to seek God's wisdom.

Rejoicing in hope;
patient in tribulation;
continuing diligently in prayer.

Romans 12:12

Ridges flow up and down the pot,
declaring the mark of the potter,
the path his hands have taken.
With each touch, the potter imparts
some of himself in the clay:
in the bend of a spout, the turn of a rim,
or an imprint on a handle.
Because the vessel bears his mark,
it is recognized as one of his and his alone.

Likewise, we should be identified as one of
God's by His mark upon us.

"By this all men will know

that you are my disciples,

if you love one another."

John 13:35

29

Uniqueness is the result, not made in a mold. No two vessels are alike, their design sometimes vastly different but each uniquely sculpted to fulfill its own specific purpose. None is insignificant.

"…Shall what is formed say to him who formed it, 'Why did you make me like this?' Does not the potter have the right to make out of the same lump of clay some pottery for noble purposes and some for common use?"

Romans 9:20-21

Not that I speak in respect of want; for I have learned,
in whatever state I am, in this to be content.

Philippians 4:11

Learning to be content could be the most difficult task we ever face. It can be like a wound that infects the entire body. However, contentment shouldn't be confused with being sedentary. A restless spirit could be God trying to move us forward.

Therefore, since we are surrounded by such
a great cloud of witnesses, let us throw off
everything that hinders and the sin that so easily
entangles, and let us run with perseverance
the race marked out for us. Let us fix our eyes
on Jesus, the author and perfecter of our faith,
who for the joy set before him endured the cross,
scorning its shame, and sat down at the right
hand of the throne of God.

Hebrews 12:1-2

Consider him who endured such opposition from sinful men,
so that you will not grow weary and lose heart.

Hebrews 12:3

And we know that in all things God works
for the good of those who love him, who have
been called according to his purpose.

Romans 8:28

Tools are used to sculpt and to cut away that which isn't needed.

-a rib (once made from real bone) used to remove excess clay and to offer extra support,

35

-sponges from the Mediterranean Sea to smooth and refine,

-and a needle to remove an uneven rim.

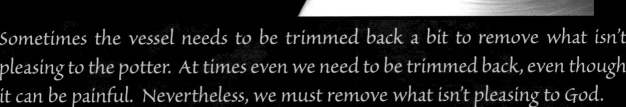

Sometimes the vessel needs to be trimmed back a bit to remove what isn't pleasing to the potter. At times even we need to be trimmed back, even though it can be painful. Nevertheless, we must remove what isn't pleasing to God.

"I am the true vine and my father is the gardener.
He cuts off every branch in me that bears no
fruit, while every branch that does bear fruit he
prunes so that it will be even more fruitful."

Just as in life – some problems can arise –
problems that could have been minute if caught early.
Other problems were there from the beginning and
surfaced over time.

Woe to those who go to great depths
to hide their plans from the Lord,
who do their work in darkness and think,
"Who sees us? Who will know?" You turn
things upside down, as if the potter were
thought to be like clay! Shall what is
formed say to him who formed it, "He did not
make me"? Can the pot say of the potter,
"He knows nothing"?

Isaiah 29:15-16

While still flexible, if the pottery becomes dented,
it can be fixed with some effort.

But other times…

…it comes crashing…

...completely down.

But the pot he was shaping from the clay was marred in his hands; so the potter formed it into another pot, shaping it as seemed best to him. Then the word of the Lord came to me: "O house of Israel, can I not do with you as the potter does?" declares the Lord. "Like clay in the hand of the potter, so are you in my hand, O house of Israel. If at any time I announce that a nation or kingdom is to be uprooted, torn down and destroyed, and if that nation I warned repents of its evil, then I will relent and not inflict on it the disaster I had planned. And if at another time I announce that a nation or kingdom is to be built up and planted, and if it does evil in my sight and does not obey me, then I will reconsider the good I had intended to do for it."

Jeremiah 18:4-10

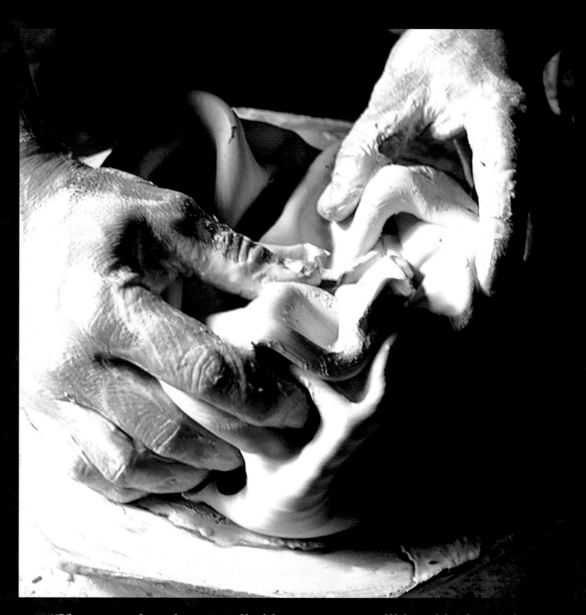

"If my people, who are called by my name, will humble themselves
and pray and seek my face and turn from their wicked ways,
then will I hear from heaven and will forgive their sin and will
heal their land."

2 Chronicles 7:14

All is not lost – there is reason to continue onward.

I sought the Lord, and he heard me, and delivered me

The clay hasn't gone anywhere, nor has its creator.

"I have told you these things, so that in me you may have peace.
In this world you will have trouble. But take heart!
I have overcome the world."

John 16:33

The potter can rewedge, rework, reinvigorate, purify, organize to a purpose, and start over again.

Therefore, if any man be in Christ, he is a new creation; old things are passed away; behold, all things are become new.

2 Corinthians 5:17

The potter can remake that which once was damaged and appeared ruined.

For God did not give us a spirit of timidity, but a spirit of power, of love, and of self-discipline.

2 Timothy 1:7

A marred vessel is remade for a useful purpose. The potter does not toss it aside. He knows his intentions and continues to mold it to his way with great anticipation for the future. Neither will God abandon us, even in the midst of our failures.

So, then, every one of us shall give account of himself to God.

Romans 14:12

Let us not become weary in doing good; for at the proper
time we will reap a harvest if we do not give up.

Galatians 6:9

Be very careful, then, how you live - not as unwise but as wise,
making the most of every opportunity, because the days are evil.

Ephesians 5:15-16

At last, the time has come to set the piece aside to dry. This is something that the potter must allow the piece to do properly and completely.

When the clay is ready, the potter will continue on with the next step.

Attachments to a vessel, such as a handle, require roughing
the surface and pressure to weld the two pieces together.
Eventually they become inseparable, fused as one.

Who shall separate us from the love of Christ? Shall trouble or hardship or persecution
or famine or nakedness or danger or sword? As it is written: "For your sake we face
death all day long; we are considered as sheep to be slaughtered." No, in all these things
we are more than conquerors through him who loved us…

…For I am convinced that neither death nor life, neither angels nor demons, neither the present nor the future, nor any powers, neither height nor depth, nor anything else in all creation, will be able to separate us from the love of God that is in Christ Jesus our Lord.

Romans 8:35-39

The potter signs his work, claiming it as his own.

Being confident of this, that he who began a good work in you
will carry it on to completion until the day of Christ Jesus.

Philippians 1:6

But we have this treasure in jars of clay to show that this all-surpassing power is from God and not from us. We are hard pressed on every side, but not crushed; perplexed, but not in despair; persecuted, but not abandoned; struck down, but not destroyed.

2 Corinthians 4:7-9

Pottery left unfired remains fragile.
The vessel is therefore fired for the first time to a bisque state
so that it can withstand the further preparation to come
— the glazing.

Therefore put on the full armor of God, so that when the day of evil comes, you may be able to stand your ground, and after you have done everything, to stand.

Ephesians 6:13

The potter takes great care to finish the inside of the pot as well as the outside. Initially the glazes do not appear as their true color. Only the potter knows the end result.

For we walk by faith, not by sight.

2 Corinthians 5:7

The glazes, when fired, will transform into a beautiful, hard coating for the pottery.

What shall we then say to these things?
If God be for us, who can be against us?

Romans 8:31

Pottery is once again placed into the kiln. The door is bricked closed, sealing the vessels within. Allowed to warm slowly, the intensity of heat builds over many long hours until the high temperature turns the glaze materials to glass.

When thro' fiery trials thy pathway shall lie,
My grace, all sufficient, shall be thy supply;
The flame shall not hurt thee; I only design
Thy dross to consume, and thy gold to refine.

"How Firm a Foundation" John Rippon

Through a small opening of the kiln a single pyrometric cone is watched closely. When it bends, it informs the potter that the kiln has reached the desired temperature.
The firing is finished.

In the midst of our trials of desperation we may not understand the hardships we endure, but we must remember the one whose promises we have trusted in the past to now lead us through.

And be not conformed to this world, but be ye transformed by the renewing of your mind, that ye may prove what is that good, and acceptable, and perfect, will of God.

Romans 12:2

"See, I have refined you, though not as silver; I have tested you in the furnace of affliction."

Isaiah 48:10

"But he knows the way that I take; when he has tested me, I will come forth as gold."

Job 23:10

The firing process cannot be rushed – warming the kiln, reaching a maturation temperature, and the necessary cool down time – a total of three days. Now it is opened to reveal the finished pieces. Works of art, manifested over a long period of time, are now completed. Pleased with his creation, the potter at last holds a vessel that will endure throughout generations.

Now to him who is able to do immeasurably more than all we ask or imagine, according to his power that is at work within us, to him be glory in the church and in Christ Jesus throughout all generations, for ever and ever. Amen.

Ephesians 3:20-21

Thou hast turned for me my mourning into dancing;
Thou hast put off my sackcloth, and girded me with gladness,
to the end that my glory may sing praise to thee, and not be silent.
Oh Lord, my God, I will give thanks unto thee forever.

Psalm 30:11-12

Ponderings…

Pottery wheels began to be used in Egypt around 3200 B.C. By 1900 B.C. pottery wheels were used in Palestine. Wheels involved a stone in a pit dug out in a dirt floor. For large pieces an assistant would lie on the floor and move the stone with his feet while the potter formed the clay from above.

Unwedged clay under a microscope is like a pile of razor blades turned in all directions.

The potter's house was a common scene in those days. Was Jeremiah sent there because the potter was "available"? We're not often available to people.

And why to the potter's house? … Where would God send us today? … To an artist? … To be in the presence of someone who knows their task, no matter how small, and is intent upon it? … To the church? … To someone who is using their gift? … Where?

During the glaze firing, a pot of one color can affect the colors of other nearby pieces.

Created in His likeness (image) to be creative ourselves – artistic by nature. Be careful what you make – it will be around for a long time.

If you were a piece of pottery, perhaps you'd be:
- a coffee mug: In the service of one individual (parent, spouse, child) who needs all your energy.
- a jar: Storage for a wealth of knowledge and experience. People come to you for advice and intuition.
- a vase: Just for looks? Or a leader who stands tall.
- a teapot: Full of warmth, love, comfort, and support.
- a serving bowl: Gregarious… You let others fill up their plate.
- none of these: A lump of clay; ill-formed, without purpose; life out of control; you've deviated; perhaps once you were a useful vessel but things happened; – or – perhaps God is just now calling you.

Remember, it is never too late and God never gives up!

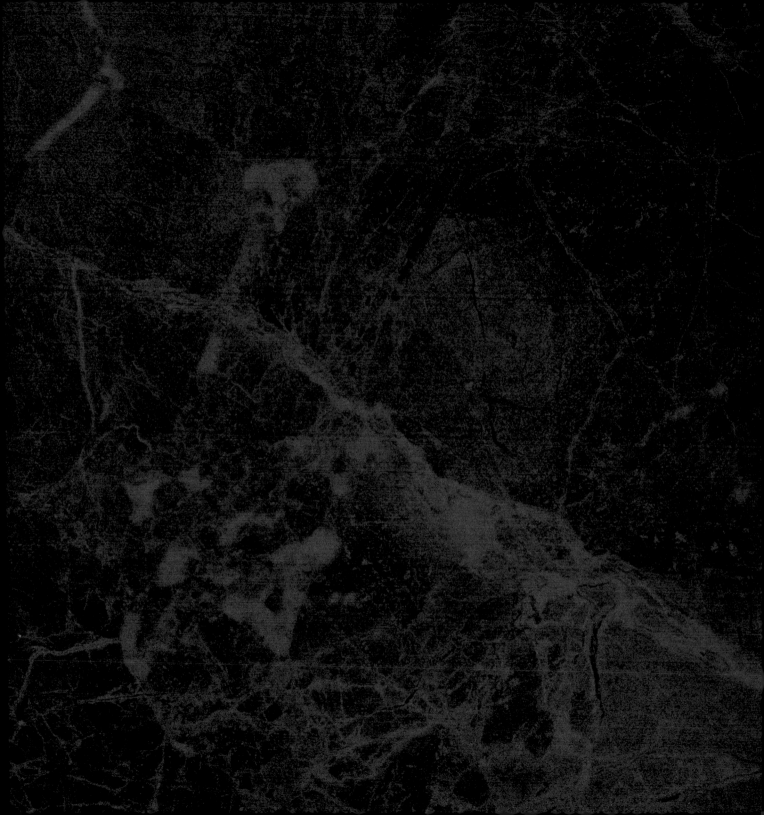

Printed in the United States
By Bookmasters